The Sign of Jonah

The Sign of Jonah

A Play in Nine Scenes

Guenter Rutenborn

Translated from the German by
George White

DIP Dramatic Insights Publications
Burien, Washington 98166

© 2005 by Dramatic Insights Publications

Published by Dramatic Insights Publications, an imprint of
Hollywood Jesus Books
P.O. Box 48282, Burien, WA 98166
http://www.hjbooks.com

Printed in the United States of America

This play is subject to royalty. Applications for license can be made
through Hollywood Jesus Books. Direct inquiries to the address listed
above or email: dramaroyalties@hjbooks.com

Library of Congress Control Number: 2005921761

Cover images courtesy of the National Oceanic and Atmospheric
Administration (NOAA / Stan Butler) and the United States National
Archives.

Dramatic Insights Publications is an independent and authorized
publishing imprint for writers working through Dramatic Insights
Ministries. Visit:
                    http://www.dramatic-insights.org

Hollywood Jesus Books is an independent and authorized print
publisher for writers published online by:
                    http://www.hollywoodjesus.com

...he began to say, "This generation is an evil generation; it seeks a sign, but no sign shall be given to it except the sign of Jonah. For as Jonah became a sign to the men of Nineveh, so will the Son of man be to this generation. The queen of the South will arise at the judgment with the men of this generation and condemn them; for she came from the ends of the earth to hear the wisdom of Solomon, and behold, something greater than Solomon is here. The men of Nineveh will arise at the judgment with this generation and condemn it; for they repented at the preaching of Jonah, and behold, something greater than Jonah is here."

Luke 11:29-32, RSVB

Contents

Publisher's Note

This edition of Guenter Rutenborn's *The Sign of Jonah* has been published in order to make available to the public, once again, a vital and dramatic argument of the traditional Christian view of theodicy: that is, the Biblical answer to the question, "Why does God allow suffering?"

Rutenborn's play, set in post-reconstruction Berlin, passed into the public domain after its original copyright lapsed. With that passing, the play also became unavailable to the public. But the play is perhaps even more relevant today than when it was first published in the United States in 1960.

Dramatic Insights Publications is pleased to have "rediscovered" Rutenborn's play, and is glad to be able to offer audiences its insights into the human condition.

Cast of Characters

(In order of appearance)

THE JUDGE

JONAH, THE PROPHET

A MAN IN THE AUDIENCE

MERCHANT

GABRIEL ⎤
MICHAEL ⎬ ARCHANGELS
RAPHAEL ⎦

THE AVERAGE MAN

THE QUEEN OF THE SOUTH, BABYLON, NINEVEH

THE AVERAGE WOMAN

STAGE MANAGER

The action is set in a theatre in West Berlin.

The time is now.

The curtain rises. The stage is in complete darkness while the house lights are still on. When the house lights finally dim, we can make out Jonah and the Judge sitting on the bench to the right of center stage, talking to each other as if unaware the curtain is up.

In the very center of the stage is a sort of pulpit which also serves as the Judge's bench. Otherwise the stage is bare. Elaborate costumes are not required. Jonah is dressed in yellow oilcloth, a raincoat, and a sweater. The Judge, and, later, the Archangels wear long robes of rather sober colors, and the upper part of their faces are masked. Whenever the characters step out of their historical parts, they remove their masks and are thus recognizable as our contemporaries. Only the Queen is costumed, according to the Revelation to John 17:4.

Scene One

Judge	What do you mean, you don't want to?
Jonah	There's no point to it.
Judge	The audience is here; the performance must go on as scheduled. You can't just decide at the last moment...
Jonah	Of course I can. I don't want to. I just don't want to.
Judge	Aha! Exactly like the biblical Jonah. He didn't want to, either.
Jonah	Precisely unlike the biblical Jonah. He, at least, *was* successful. He *was* able to convert a great city.
Judge	Yet he did it reluctantly; he wasn't at all pleased that Nineveh became converted.
Jonah	And I'm not pleased that the people today refuse to become converted. The world has been turned upside-down, everything is completely topsy-turvy, only the people haven't changed. Everything has remained the same.

Judge   The more reason for us to perform tonight.

Jonah   Perform? Before whom? Do you really think we have the right audience?

Judge   Signs do occur. They don't necessarily depend upon an audience.

Jonah   Oh, the public has changed. Yes, when our cities were heaps of rubble the people seemed different. But now that the cities are almost entirely rebuilt, do you think that they still remember—or even want to be reminded of those days when fire and destruction rained from the skies? Today, wherever you look, you only see those... those neon lights.

Judge   But even now, sometimes, when clearing away left-over debris they find duds...

Jonah   Duds! Oh yes, duds! Then there's a big commotion, lots of excitement, talk. The police rope off the area, the entire neighborhood is evacuated. But when human remains are discovered among the rubble it is removed in the dark of night. Secretly. So no one will be offended. No! Nowadays we're far too concerned with the living, and not at all with the dead. Life today is far too noisy for my taste. Too many cars, portable radios, portable TVs. But the dead—for whom I'm supposed to speak here tonight—the dead are silent. Silent and helpless.

Judge   I don't believe that. Let me tell you something. No, the people haven't forgotten. Listen. In 1954, in December, I went to London, to root for our National Team in the soccer match against

	England. On the trip back, near Louvain, the engine jumped the tracks, rolled down the embankment and pulled along the first three cars. I was in one.
Jonah	You? You were in that wreck?
Judge	Well, yes. But it isn't the accident itself I want to talk about.
Jonah	It must have been horrible.
Judge	Not worse that what happened to you in that submarine. No, I shouldn't even mention both in one breath. You were the sole survivor. I was one of about twenty...
Jonah	Twenty? Only... about twenty? Not more?
Judge	Well, forgive me for using the blunt language of men who've survived disaster. Yes, one of about twenty. But as I said before, it isn't the accident I want to talk about. What I do want you to know is what happened when we arrived in Aachen. There was a big crowd waiting—journalists, reporters. One of the reporters, he was from the North German Broadcasting Company—strange, isn't it, that such unimportant details cling to your mind?—was utterly amazed at the way we expressed ourselves when he asked us if there had been a panic, whether the people had been very frightened...
Jonah	Which car did you say you were in?
Judge	The third. It rolled down the embankment and crashed on top of the second.
Jonah	Horrible.

Judge   Well, yes. But to get back to the reporter. He almost refused to believe us when we told him that the passengers remained completely calm.

Jonah   Calm?! Why, that's incredible!

Judge   But true. I often wondered about it, until much later a psychologist explained it to me. We were able to remain calm, he said, because we had been conditioned by our experiences during the war. So you see, the memories have remained alive. Very much alive, in spite of neon lights and the enthusiasm for soccer. I've no doubt that the audience still remembers. So go ahead, start the play!

Jonah   (Turning around and pretending to see AUDIENCE for first time) Which, of course, we've already done, Ladies and Gentlemen.

Judge   (Also facing the AUDIENCE) The bit with the open curtain was the first trick.

Jonah   The first trick. Yes. The first of several.

In the audience, a man rises most indignantly.

Trick   Trick! What is this? A circus? I was under the impression I would see a serious play, a biblical play. That's what you advertised in the papers, didn't you? Well, that's why I'm here. But "trick"—trick? I'm leaving, I want my money back...

Judge   You are seeing a biblical play. Please... ! Why don't you stay, Mister...

Trick   Trick. My name's Trick.

Judge   Ah, Mister Trick. A pleasure, indeed a pleasure. All right, then, to begin. (Pointing at JONAH) This is Jonah. You've heard of Jonah, haven't you? Jonah, one of the minor prophets.

Trick   Jonah? Oh yes. Isn't he the one who allegedly was swallowed by a whale?

Judge   Yes, absolutely correct. The one from the Bible, who later went to Nineveh to preach about death and resurrection. Perhaps you're familiar with the story.

Trick   Yes, yes, I seem to remember now. Not too clearly though. (Sits)

Judge   Well, that's forgivable. It happened a very long time ago, and such things are difficult to substantiate. This sort of submersion went unreported in the press. But our Jonah, as you've just heard, immersed himself not only in the problems of our age but also in prophecy. (Gesturing to JONAH) Jonah, if you please.

JUDGE exits and the curtain falls, but JONAH has stepped out in front of it, and very casually sits down on the edge of the proscenium.

Scene Two

Jonah   Yes, I'm Jonah. The Jonah who was swallowed by a whale. Well, actually, this is what really happened. During the last war, when I was in command of a submarine...

Trick   (Rising again) Submarine! I was led to believe you're the Prophet Jonah.

Merchant (Sitting in the back of the AUDIENCE calls out) Quiet up front! (Trick sits again)

Jonah   It's imperative only for a man to identify himself with a fact, with a certain matter, with an occurrence. Let me explain. Well, as I said before, during the Second World War, I was in command of a submarine. We were cruising on the surface when suddenly we were attacked by a bomber, and we had to crash dive. Something went wrong. We hit bottom. We couldn't move. We were stuck. Needless to say, the engineer tried everything possible; it was of no avail. We were doomed to the slow death of suffocation. I venture to say that suffocation is the most horrible form of death—but then, I suppose, one's own death usually is the most horrible. "What's going to happen to us?" the crew kept asking over and over again, a little more desperate each time. "You'll die!" I finally shouted angrily. "To die is part of your job!" The engineer sneered, "Why not try prayers?" "We'd rather curse," the men shouted back. And curse they did. I don't suppose I have to tell you how adept sailors are at cursing. But after a while even the cursing stopped, for strange as it may seem, no one can go on cursing indefinitely. "Now only a miracle can pry us loose," said the engineer. He said many more things, and then he began to cry, very softly. Tears are catching. Soon others were crying too. But again, there's no need to go into details. Suffice it to say that on the average, they were rather young lads, and they cried for their dear ones. As for myself, I was rather apathetic. When they kept asking me how I felt, I became annoyed and shouted, "I'm praying!" It wasn't the truth. Well, before long, the thing I had dreaded most did happen. One of the men committed suicide. The engineer. Everyone panicked. I suppose that's only natural. There is something horrifying about sharing a stifling hot tinfish with a corpse. We were also beginning to feel the lack of oxygen. If you further keep in mind the slow, monotonous fashion in which time passed, then you'll understand that before long I had to cope with a virtual epidemic of suicides. I was powerless. I couldn't be everywhere at once, and furthermore, the lack of oxygen made rapid movement imprudent. At long last there were only two of us left. By a strange coincidence the other man's name was Abel, Abel Moeller. Abel, by the way, is a Hebrew name. Well, Abel had discovered one last oxygen tank just as we thought the end had come. "I'm going to live," he shouted excitedly. A most foolish thing to do, getting excited when there's so precious little oxygen. I tried my best to calm him down. "Easy, son, easy," I said, but Abel had reached for a revolver and was aiming at me. The pistol jammed. He began to sob and threw himself into my arms and begged for forgiveness. "All right," I told him, "release the oxygen. We'll see who'll suffocate first. God, in whom neither of us believes, shall be our judge!" We sat down next to each other. He was crying and I—I suddenly found the strength to pray. I prayed very quietly, very calmly. You can guess what for. Right! To make the oxygen last a little longer. Then the sobbing next to me began to peter out. Suddenly Abel flung out his arms in a violent spasm, his skin turned dark, almost purple... no, I'd just as soon spare you the gory details. God had judged him and taken no heed of his tears of remorse.

I fell to my knees and in a choking voice I vowed, "If you'll let me survive I shall become Your witness!"—then I tried the valves once again— you know, the valves that regulate the pressurized air that forces water out of the diving chambers. "In the name of the Lord," I shouted,

15

"flee, you evil spirits of the deep!" I heard a vicious, angry hissing—yes, vicious and angry! But it sounded to me like a chorus of angels' voices!

(He now stands up) Well, as you can see, I'm here, and now I call myself Jonah. And why not? Whether submarine or whale, hell is always one and the same. As a matter of fact, much, very much, always remains one and the same. Jonah tells the venerable, somewhat juvenile tale that he had gone to Nineveh to preach about death and resurrection. Nineveh! Why Nineveh? After all today, this evening, we are in Berlin. In our playlet, even while the performance goes on, Nineveh becomes Babylon, by which Saint John, whose Revelations are our source, meant Rome. Yes, one must know the original texts. It is important to know the original texts. And what is in a name? Does the name really matter? Nineveh, Berlin, Babylon, Rome... tomorrow it might be New York, Moscow... who knows. Ah, but the original texts! Take this quotation, for example: mene, mene, tekel upharsin.

He pretends to notice that the AUDIENCE *does not understand the meaning of the saying.*

Jonah   I beg your pardon? Oh, you're not familiar with that quotation? A pity. A real pity! (Pointing at AUDIENCE) And you're the ones to be pitied. One should have understood its meaning long ago—after all, at one time it was a commonly used expression in Germany. The original menetekel—that too, by the way, is Hebrew—was written in fiery letters into the walls of Belshazzar's banquet hall, just, as a lot more recently, it was written across the width and breadth of our country. It means—and hasn't it truly come to pass?—it means numbered, numbered, weighed and divided. If you're interested in the full story you can read it in the book written by my colleague Daniel. But we had better stick with Jonah, the Prophet Jonah, with the sign of Jonah!

He snaps his fingers, to indicate that the curtain is to be raised and also that the lights are to go on.

Scene Three

The judge enters again, followed by the ARCHANGELS
GABRIEL, MICHAEL, and RAPHAEL.)

Judge   I have agreed to enact the part of the Judge.
According to latest research there exists, besides
the Archangels... (Pointing at them) these three
here... a well substantiated, old tradition of an
angel who sits in Judgment. I have agreed to
enact that part since I had ample opportunity to
get to know a large segment of our present-day
nations. I was in Italy—in uniform, not as a
tourist—then in North Africa. Oh yes, I became
well-acquainted with the charming Italians and
the honorable Africans—and I learned to respect
the British. Close to the end of the war I fell into
French captivity. The French! I learned to hate
them! Yes, I hated them as passionately as I had
once loved and revered them. Then I was turned
over to the Russians. At first I hated the
Russians, but soon they persuaded me to love
them. As for the Germans whom I had loved all
my life, I learned to hold them in deepest
contempt, because...

Jonah	(Stepping toward him) Enough already! Enough! We're not concerned with your private life and opinions. You're the Judge. We expect you to be severe, but impartial. It is your duty to weigh all nations according to one inflexible standard of justice.
Gabriel	I'm supposed to represent the Archangel Gabriel. Gabriel means "God is my strength." I'm here neither as the sole survivor from a U-boat, nor as a repatriate from Siberia. But I was in Dresden when the Yanks paid us a flying visit. Buried alive in a basement for ten days I was. Has any one of you experienced Dresden?

He pauses for a moment.

Gabriel	Let me tell you, it was deliberate murder. Dastardly murder.
Jonah	Quiet! Quiet! The part of the Judge is not played by you but by Mister.... (He gives the real name of actor playing JUDGE; then, to the AUDIENCE) Well, he's also a survivor.
Michael	And my name is Michael. Translated that means, "Who is like God?" A question like that shouldn't really be asked, should it? You're bound to get a stupid answer. You know what I mean, don't you?
	(He gives the Hitler salute)
	As for myself, well, the Amis interned me at the Dachau concentration camp. Yes, you heard right, the Amis, the Americans. They beat us and kept us on a near-starvation diet. Me, of all

people. For this nonsense...

(He gives Hitler salute)

was something for which for a long time already I felt nothing but contempt. As a matter of fact, that was the reason I wound up with a penal company assigned to carry out mass executions in the East. But only of inferior races. Well, don't think for a moment it was a pleasant job we had...

Jonah   (To AUDIENCE) Another survivor! (To RAPHAEL) Next, please.

Raphael   My name is Raphael. It means simply—if you'll pardon the expression—"Heil God!"

Jonah   Another survivor, without doubt.

Raphael   You bet. Escaped from East Prussia, crossed the Baltic on a small fishing vessel, bombed, strafed...

Gabriel   You're tugging at my heart strings. Ah, cut it out! Are you trying to impress me, a veteran of Dresden?

Raphael   Afterwards, somewhere in Pomerania, I was stood up against a wall... and executed.

Michael   What?

Raphael   They missed, naturally! They were stinking drunk, otherwise I'd be a real angel by now.

Jonah   (Shaking his head doubtfully and amusedly) Well, well, well...

Michael   I've been saying it all along: we're not angels.

Jonah   Yes, it is rather indisputable that we Germans

	never had any excessive relations with angels; rather with the opposite number.
Raphael	See Goethe's *Faust*!
Michael	And Thomas Mann's *Doctor Faustus*.
Jonah	All right, all right; let's get started.
Raphael	The sonorous sun, in ancient fashion In song match-joins the brother spheres...
Jonah	Hey! Not that! Cut it out! (Contemptuously) Classicist!
Raphael	I merely wanted to prove that there are angels in *Faust*.
Jonah	Cut out the gibberish. Get down to business. Begin.
Raphael	Begin? Where?
Jonah	At the conclusion.

When RAPHAEL pretends not to understand, the JUDGE steps into the center.

Judge	With Judgment Day. For Judgment Day is at hand. The destruction of Babylon, alias Rome, alias Dresden, alias Berlin, alias Coventry, alias Rotterdam, alias Hiroshima, alias Nagasaki, et cetera, proves it. The spirits of the lower depths have risen, the Atom bombs are ready...
Raphael	And the H-bombs...
Gabriel	And Cobalt bombs...
Jonah	(Teasingly) Mustn't forget the flying saucers. Anything else?
Judge	Stick to the issue at hand, please! (He takes his

position behind his desk. To the AUDIENCE) We
request your presence on Judgment Day.
Trumpets please!

Trumpets play a fanfare.

Judge   The Court in the Sign of Jonah is now in session!

*Everyone takes his place, the ARCHANGELS come to center
stage, JONAH, somewhat watchful, always ready to comment
or interrupt, remains slightly to right.*

Michael   The Day of Judgment dawns
           And thus the Lord commands his will:
           Now let the sun stand still
           As once it stood for Joshua
           In the Valley of Ajalon.
           Let purity in its own bright light,
           Like a grand prophetic vision, shimmer,
           The day shall never change again to night.

Gabriel   When the lower depths belched smoke
           To stay the newly risen day,
           When flames of Hell turned night
           Into a blinding noon,
           Then was the abyss opened—
           The final change evoked;
           Then came destruction
           In which God's own work must end.

Raphael   Come closer then, you purest works of God.
           Give all your beauty to this one great day.
           The black abyss in you shall be eclipsed,
           And suffering, and all the earth's dismay
           Shall come in time to face

The one eternal light.

Angels   So we praise Thee for this very terror's sake.
          Hell's fury rages—dies.
          Here ends a world in tears.
          And after all its cries of pain have faded,
          That last day's sun will rise.

Michael   Babylon is fallen,
          And with it pomp and blasphemy.
          Babylon is fallen!
          Earth need no longer serve in hate,
          The curse is broken, the night takes flight.

Gabriel   The world has not been shattered
          The sighs on sinful lips will praise him still.
          On Babel's black parched walls that burned,
          Still rest the shadows of God's strength.

Raphael   Let even those who fall kneel yet again to pray
          And know that God's unbounded beauty
          Can stay the threat of death.
          And from this certainty, this new found truth,
          Shall they, the fallen, find new hope.

Angels   You, who counted time in solemn circles,
          Now laud the justice of the universe.
          You are the world's order and its ornament
          Let God's house tremble with your song.
          In you shall the fallen see
          That in God's hand lie death and resurrection.

Jonah   Nicely said, gentlemen, very nicely indeed. We
          are indebted to you. But you did say your piece
          "sub species aeternitatis" and it is rather doubtful
          if anyone in these hectic times can permit himself
          the luxury of accepting the long-range view, the

point of view of eternity.

The QUEEN OF BABYLON, the AVERAGE MAN, the AVERAGE WOMAN are coming down the aisle, obviously in answer to the ARCHANGELS' invitation.

Jonah   Ah, here are three people who have accepted your invitation. (Aside to the JUDGE) Well, we'll see who's right.

The QUEEN OF BABYLON, THE AVERAGE MAN, and the AVERAGE WOMAN have come on stage.

Scene Four

Judge   (To JONAH) You seem to be ill qualified for the legal profession. You merely look at people and immediately form prejudices. Snap judgments. Very bad. I recall having read somewhere that you practiced law in Nineveh without ever arriving at a proper verdict. Snap judgments, prejudices. We shall have to reexamine these cases.

Jonah   What do you mean prejudices? You completely fail to appreciate prophetic insight. Just take an unhurried look at these three. Look at their faces. They are faces from the twentieth century— certainly one of the strangest of all centuries. Well, is there another more weighted down with guilt and blood, and at the same time filled with excuses and self-justifications? The face of twentieth-century man! Hmmm! You can pick out that face from all the faces of all the centuries that have been. Only rarely will you find, combined in one face, so much cruelty, self-righteousness and emptiness, while at the same time devoid of all religious feelings. I'm willing to bet that none of those three have the slightest notion where they are...

Judge   You're forgetting yourself, prophet.

Jonah   Who can't forget himself must never become a prophet.

Judge   Nevertheless we must adhere to an orderly legal procedure. (To the newcomers) We are in your debt for accepting our solemn invitation. The court has decided to simplify proceedings by reducing the innumerable counts of indictment to one special case. The Court requests you hold yourselves available as witnesses.

Man   Witness? Witness my foot. I'm here as a plaintiff!

Jonah   (To JUDGE) You see! I've been saying it all along.

Judge   (To AVERAGE MAN) You're entitled to voice your complaints within the framework of your testimony as a witness, provided of course you pay strict attention to truth and objectivity. (To everyone, dryly) All right, then! Disregarding the numerous inexcusable crimes committed in the City of Nineveh, alias Babylon or Babel, alias Rome I, II, III, et cetera, et cetera, the Court will confine its examinations to the initial case of guilt of the City: its inhabitants and government, respectively. We shall consider the well-known, precedent-setting, political case of the three men cast alive into the furnace of fire. See exhibit one, the Book of Daniel, Chapter Three. It is a reasonable assumption that our witnesses are familiar with the matter, since at least one billion copies of the Bible have been printed in a thousand or so languages and dialects. (To the QUEEN) Just in case it has slipped your mind, my dear lady, I will summarize the facts once again. In the year 602 before Christ—*before* Christ, though I must emphasize most emphatically that this is not to be construed as a mitigating circumstance—well, in that year 602 an incident occurred in your city which must be considered the origin of the misfortune which brought about the complete destruction of your city, the capital of the world, through the fires of hell. *You* were responsible for the construction of a furnace into which were cast alive three respected and well-liked men, to wit, the witnesses Shadrach, Meshach, and Abednego. This is a crime against humanity.

Raphael   Correction, Your Honor. Though the three gentlemen were cast into the furnace of flaming fire, I was sent to protect them from serious bodily harm. They survived the ordeal and later were appointed to high administrative offices.

Queen   And this incident did not occur during my reign. The power-drunk Nebuchadnezzar gave the order.

Judge   What the blazes! What sort of excuse is that? My dear lady, in another minute you shall be properly identified. In his Revelation, Saint John supplies us with your criminal warrant. (To MICHAEL) Michael, please read the warrant to the Court.

Michael   (Reading from a book) The word of the Lord:

"The woman was dressed in purple and scarlet, and glittered with gold, precious stones, and pearls. She had in her hand a gold cup..."

Queen   The cup! Oh, I left it at home. It was too much of a bother...

Man   What a dope! Now you've given yourself away.

Jonah   Yes, sweetheart, that wasn't very clever.

Judge   And that gold cup contains the very proof. For it was full of... full of... Michael!

Michael "Full of accursed things, and the impurities of her immorality and drunkenness." By the way, by drunkenness is meant, "drunk with the blood of God's people."

Judge   (To the QUEEN) Well, there's the proof! Or perhaps you cling to the belief that burning alive is not bloodshed? (To the AUDIENCE) Ladies and Gentlemen, there is one point you all must be absolutely clear about. This Court is more precise than is customary in the court of law, even if our methods of inquiry into the mythological and original precedent might seem somewhat unusual. However, this Court will at no time tolerate de-mythologizing, or any other excuses, or claims of misunderstandings.

Jonah   Hear! Hear!

Judge   The Court is not afflicted with a "Psychology of the Superficial." The court knows precisely the standards it must adhere to. (To the QUEEN) You, Madame, have agreed to enact tonight the part of the Queen. At another time you're Medea, or

	Portia, or Margaret. Actually there's no need for these disguises, no one is fooled. We know exactly who is hiding behind all these masks. Whether you're enacting the Queen of Babylon or, on the other hand, the Queen of the South, we know that in reality you're Miss.... (He names the real name of actress playing QUEEN)
Queen	Mister.... (She gives the real name of actor playing JUDGE) Have you suddenly gone mad? I thought we're playing...
Judge	Playing? You're *playing*? I reject the term, playing. I reject it most adamantly. We judge. We sit in judgment over our age, and after all, you are a woman of the twentieth century!
Queen	Yes.
Judge	You agreed to enact the part of the Queen?
Queen	What else would I be doing here?
Judge	Your insolence makes it absolutely impossible to give favorable consideration to your protests. Now then! To create a character on stage demands a complete identification with that character, doesn't it? The more complete, the better.
Jonah	Friends, let's not waste time with such trivia. Otherwise we'll lay an egg tonight and the author will get blamed.
Judge	(To JONAH) The Court doesn't think the author matters right now. What does matter is that we clarify this point. (To QUEEN) Now, Miss.... (He names her real name) since you are unable to

31

identify yourself with such a character as the Queen of Babylon, it follows that you, as a woman of the twentieth century, are capable to *be* that bloodthirsty queen. After all, if you can't identify yourself with the queen you'll present an absolutely implausible, unconvincing character tonight. Correct?

Queen   Oh, this is a horrible play.

Judge   You're not to judge the play. That privilege is reserved for the audience and the reviewers. All that is expected of you is a creditable performance.

Gabriel   (To QUEEN) I can't see why you're getting all hepped up, Miss…. (He names her real name). All right, at the suggestion of Guenter Rutenborn we're concerned with the old story of the three men and the furnace of fire. Well? Didn't we have furnaces of fire? Didn't we cast innocent people into the flames? Everyone knows we did.

Jonah   That is also my contention. The translation of the Hebrew text into German makes for an interesting parallel.

Michael   It has also been translated into every other language.

Raphael   You certainly find furnaces of fire elsewhere.

Judge   We're not concerned with that. We're dealing with the Hebrew-German precedent alone. By examining the case of the three men and the furnace of fire in an incendiary Babylon—or whatever the name might be—we will be forced to consider other burnt out cities and their

32

incendiaries—the original incendiaries, if you please. Let us proceed with the investigation.

The AVERAGE WOMAN has been trying to catch the JUDGE'S attention; now she does.

Judge   Yes!

Woman   Your Honor, please, may I have the floor, Your Honor! I'm what's usually called just an average housewife. You know what I mean. But I like to think that now I'm speaking for all the mothers. Yes, the mothers! Unsung heroes they are, mothers, suffering the agonies of giving birth, and raising their children with love and worry and fear, only to have a cruel world take them away. Shadrach, Meshach and Abednego! They're my sons! Even today I remember how they promised to fulfill our great hopes in them. Oh, it wasn't easy, raising them. Just think, Your Honor, three boys at one time...

Judge   All right, my good woman, all right. Please, confine yourself to answering questions. Do you happen to know how it came about that your sons were arrested and condemned to suffer such a terrible fate?

Woman   Do I know! Of course I know! Don't these things always happen the same way? Someone denounced them. You see, Your Honor, there was this decree. And everyone was supposed to obey it. It said, everyone must salute a golden idol, and the standards and the flags. But my boys were intellectuals. It wasn't easy, Your Honor; we had

33

> to sacrifice a great deal, but I insisted the boys get a fine education.

Jonah   Well, Mom, now don't get carried away. The Hebrew original is just a little bit different. (To MICHAEL) Perhaps you can help us out once again, Michael.

MICHAEL opens his book.

Michael   "Thereupon certain Chaldeans came forward and laid an accusation against the Jews, saying to King Nebuchad-nazi—Nebuchadnezzar I meant to say (Giving the Hitler salute)—O King, may you live forever—at least a thousand years. You, O King, have made a decree that every man who hears the sound of the horn, the pipe, the lyre, and every other musical instrument, shall fall down and prostrate himself before the image of gold; and whosoever does not fall down and prostrate himself shall be cast into the midst of a furnace of flaming fire. Now, there are certain Jews..."

Judge   That'll do. Thank you. The parallel has been clearly established. (To the AVERAGE WOMAN) All right, then. Who denounced your sons?

Woman   The Queen's already implicated. But she's merely the highest authority.

She continues to look around unhurriedly, peering into the audience.

Woman   Is there anyone who at one time or another hasn't stooped to denunciation at least once?

Now she is looking straight at MICHAEL, who ducks.

Michael   What are you looking at me for? I didn't do it!

Jonah   Now don't get upset. You're supposed to behave like an angel.

Michael   But Mister.... (Giving JONAH'S real name) You know I'm not an angel.

Jonah   Well, there's no doubt about that. After all, you're a human being, and certainly guilty of some minor human transgressions.

Michael   Minor... Oh, I'm not talking about minor transgressions. It's not that harmless. Before they drafted me into the Wehrmacht I was a clerk in the municipal marriage license bureau. I can't help thinking about it... often at night I wake up in a sweat...! Must I really tell everything?

His sudden outburst has aroused the JUDGE'S curiosity.

Judge   You certainly must. This is Judgment Day. Acquit yourself!

Michael   (He deliberates for a while; then, compelled) It's a long story; it goes all the way back to the end of the First World War. That Versailles peace treaty got my goat. It was wrong, it deprived me of my West-Prussian home. When Hitler came along and denounced Versailles, I joined the party. In due time I became clerk in the marriage license bureau. I officiated at weddings and inspected the documents, the birth certificates— well, I suppose you remember why: because of the Aryan grandmothers. I had to certify that all these people had the proper racial background. Well, at first I saw no harm in differentiating between Germans and Jews. But then, later, they built the furnaces. To my great shame—to my eternal shame!—I also consigned people to the furnaces. Yes, yes I did! I'm a murderer, can't you see! A murderer! A murderer, not an angel!

Jonah   Come, come, get hold of yourself. Look...

Judge   You're stepping out of character, Mister.... (Giving MICHAEL'S real name)

Jonah   Really, my good man, really you're going too far. Just pause and think for a moment. Consider the implications of your statement. Think of the innumerable certificates of baptism issued by Christian clergymen, by municipal clerks.

Queen   (Horrified) O...! Even the author of this play...

Jonah   Yes! Himself a pastor!

During this entire exchange the AVERAGE WOMAN has been walking around the stage, looking at the actors, and then she has gone down into the audience. Now, back on stage again, she stops abruptly in front of the AVERAGE MAN.

Woman   (Screaming) Now I know! He's the one! He did it! (To the AVERAGE MAN) You denounced them!

Man   Ah, you're off your rocker. Lay off me, will you! I'm just an average man!

Woman   Don't you raise your voice. You denounced my boys. You! You! Who snapped to attention, mornings, noon, and night? Who permitted them to put a uniform on you? Who came at dawn and knocked at the doors of frightened people? Who drove the police cars? Guarded the prisons? Was the executioner? Who? Who built the furnaces? Stoked them? Who helps tyrants everywhere be tyrants? Who sells his eyes and ears for a reward? Who builds a monument to evil?

All   (Except JUDGE and JONAH) The Average Man! The Average Man!

Judge   (To the AVERAGE MAN) Ah! So we've finally caught up with you! How many nations have been destroyed by "average men"?

The AVERAGE MAN attempts to get off stage, but is prevented by the JUDGE.

Judge   Stop! Where do you think you're going? Do you really think you can escape judgment?

Man   What's the matter with you, Mister....? (Giving JUDGE'S real name) What's the big idea, bringing politics into this? A harmless one-act play, I thought. Why, what you're doing is downright vicious! (Facing the AUDIENCE) Ladies and Gentlemen, they have no right to do this to me. I was hired for the part of the "Average Man." All of a sudden they pounce on me with that political nonsense. Me! I've *been* denazified! Heck, no, I've had it. I'm going home! Lots and lots I've seen in my days, but never anything like this.

STAGE MANAGER enters.

Scene Five

Stg. Mgr. Hold it! Just a moment, Mister.... (She gives real name of actor playing AVERAGE MAN) You're ruining the entire scene. Look! (Shows him a copy of the script) It says so right here. Average Man. That's the part you've been hired for. You're the Average Man.

Man Average Man! How dare you! You're insulting my intelligence. Average Man! Some nerve! Don't you realize you're dealing with a highly educated man?

Stg. Mgr. Are you completely out of your mind? Of course I know who you really are, but tonight you're playing the "Average Man." (Facing the AUDIENCE) Will someone kindly hand me a playbill. Mister.... (Giving his real name) doesn't seem to believe me.

Man (Slapping his forehead) Holy smoke, yes! Forgive me! (Facing the AUDIENCE) Ladies and Gentlemen, this sort of thing is called surrealism. But don't you agree things are getting just a bit too realistic? They make you believe you're just playing a part—just playing, mind you—and suddenly you find the grease paint of propriety scraped off your face, and you just stand here...! Well, suppose you tell me what you would have done in my place?

Judge   Take your place on stage, Average Man!

Average Man does.

Judge   So you finally understand that you are to answer *as* the Average Man. Well, then, did you or didn't you denounce the three men?

Man   Did I or didn't I? Why ask me? I'm just an Average Man, a man of the people...

Judge   A man of all the peoples!

AVERAGE MAN meditates upon this for awhile, growing increasingly more horrified as the idea takes hold of him. Then he cries out in horror.

Man   No! No! that can't be true! Never! Never! That would be too much to bear! If that were true then, as a German, I tortured Poles and murdered Ukrainians; as a Pole I expropriated Germans; as a Ukrainian I was a murderous partisan; as an American I pulverized Dresden; as a Russian I raped and pillaged; as a Frenchman...! No, for heaven's sake, no! That's more than I can bear!

He collapses on the bench.

Woman   There you are! I sure know how to spot 'em! That hit home!

Judge   Not so fast, my good woman. Now I should like

to have the Average Man tell us who incited him to his actions. Of course we must remember that we're solely concerned with the initial precedent. Well, then, who incited the Average Man to denounce others?

Woman   Your Honor, why are you looking at me? I didn't incite anyone.

Judge   Come now, come now.

Raphael   There's no point beating around the bush. Everyone knows it was the Average Woman. In the first story ever told it was "woman." The apple, remember!

Gabriel   You're not going to drag in that old story!

Raphael   Why not? Who plucked the apple? Who gave it to Adam?

Jonah   Apple, apple! I challenge anyone to show me the passage where it is stated that it was an apple.

Michael   Apple or no apple! What's the difference? A man must pursue his career, must advance in his job. In order to get ahead he must be liked by his superiors. It's always the same story: to improve your family circumstances you must improve your position, and is there any more sure fire way of doing that than by denouncing someone else, and thus getting a better paid job?

Woman   (To MICHAEL) You're still young. Just wait 'til you have children. You don't know how it is when you have kids. How important it becomes that the man of the house is impotent.

There is much laughter, and she, deeply embarrassed,

continues.

Woman	Important, I mean. My husband simply had to become an inspector. There were too many mouths to feed. I said that before, didn't I?
Jonah	But aren't you forgetting that one fine day your children—for whose sake you pushed your husband—wind up in a furnace of fire?
Woman	Well, they weren't my children.
Queen	Only a moment ago you *did* make yourself the spokesman for all mothers.
Woman	I did? Now I'm really getting confused.
Michael	You? Who should get you confused? But me, now take me for example. First I was responsible for sending Jews to concentration camps; later I served time in a camp myself.
Gabriel	Right. The full cycle, my good woman. The chickens come home to roost. I was a bombardier. I dropped bombs on London and Coventry, Rotterdam. Later, in Dresden, they dropped on me.
Woman	Well, actually, as far as my own children were concerned, I was very fortunate.
Jonah	We're not really concerned with your personal fate at this moment. The cycle affects each and every one of us. Neither neon lights nor portable TVs offer a solution. Therefore fear, the common fear...
Queen	You may stop right there! Things are getting a bit too explicit for comfort.

Judge   (To the QUEEN) You'd like that, wouldn't you? Because now we're getting closer to the major culprit. Who gave the orders? Who *did* make the weekly paychecks dependent upon blind obedience?

Queen   How dare you address me in such fashion. As Judge you are to carry out the laws, but it is I, the Queen, who make them!

In the back of the house the MERCHANT has risen and is coming down the aisle.

Scene Six

He is a prosperous looking, well fed and well dressed man.

Merchant Just a moment, please. Excuse me for interrupting, but there are a few questions I'd like to ask. It so happens that I'm very interested in this case. Mind if I come on stage?

Jonah Not at all. Join us. By all means.

The MERCHANT comes on stage.

Merchant I hope you'll forgive me for this intrusion. I must confess the proceedings on stage have affected me deeply.

Queen You don't look it.

Merchant Ah, Madame, please, please, you mustn't say that. Does anything today look the way it should?

Jonah (Impatiently) You said you wanted to ask some questions.

Merchant Questions! Yes, oh yes, of course, questions. I'm a merchant. At one time I had a beautiful shop. Yes, and I had my own home, and a wife and two children. I'm saying "had" advisedly, for properly

	regarded... well, how shall I put it?
Judge	I take it you're still a merchant.
Jonah	Have you lost your business?
Merchant	Well, that's just it. That's what suddenly doesn't... well, frankly, it doesn't seem right to me.

With the exception of the JUDGE and MICHAEL everyone laughs.

Michael	Come on, lay off him!
Merchant	Must I tell you that the bombs have made me a poor and lonely man. Just a moment ago it occurred to me again. Yes, we'll never be able to forget completely those days. Sometimes at night, when sleep doesn't want to come, when you toss and toss, then suddenly I see them again... my two small children, a boy and a girl... yes, and my wife, too. Oh, she was goodness personified. (To JUDGE and JONAH) And now you claim each and everyone of us is responsible for his own, horrible fate—especially we Germans. Let me state quite openly and in no uncertain terms that I cannot accept even the slightest share of this guilt. I never joined the Party—not an easy thing to do for a man engaged in trade. As a matter of fact, as a merchant I can tell you that it isn't always simple to remain honest. It's liable to lead to bankruptcy and poverty. He... (Pointing the AVERAGE MAN) had to provide for his children, therefore he had to make money. He came to the same conclusion, namely that honesty isn't

always the best policy. In order to provide properly for his children, he had to curry the favors of his superiors. We have heard in what fashion. (Pointing at AVERAGE WOMAN) The Average Woman only wanted the best for her children; so she drove them to their deaths. (Turning to AUDIENCE) Ladies and Gentlemen, what sort of world is this! Tell me! Tell me! Will someone please tell me!

Judge   Yes, what sort of world...! Miss...._ (Naming the actress playing STAGE MANAGER by her real name) please, hand us a different play. We're stuck. This play isn't suitable for our age.

STAGE MANAGER enters.

Stg. Mgr. What other play do you have in mind, Mister.... (Gives JUDGE'S real name)

Judge   Now let's see! Well, for example, we could do "Oedipus." He slew his father and committed incest with his mother... though he wasn't aware of the true relationships. Of course one would be entitled to raise the same question over again: what sort of world is this we live in.

Merchant Sounds suitable. "Oedipus." I'm not familiar with the play. But then, I'm afraid I rarely find time to read or to go to the theatre. Is it a modern play?

Queen   You mean you haven't discovered that yet?

Jonah   Have all of you gone completely out of your minds? Are you nuts? We're not here to ask questions; they've already been asked. We're here to give answers—*the* answer!

Judge	Right! We can't proceed in this fashion. (Banging gavel) Order! Order in the Court! Places! Everyone take their places. Yes, the Court cannot permit itself to become involved in digressions. Nothing must interfere with the case under examination. We are here to determine who was responsible for the murder...
Gabriel	Your Honor, it was not murder, only attempted murder!
Judge	The Court stands corrected. Very well, the responsibility for the attempted murder of the three men cast into the furnace of fire. The Court accepts the suggestion of the merchant, Mister... (To the MERCHANT) What is your name?
Merchant	Tiemann, Your Honor, Ernest Tiemann. Fruits and Vegetables, Wholesale. (Hands judge his business card, around which is wrapped a crisp bank note)
Judge	(Taking the bribe) The Court accepts the... suggestion of Mister Tiemann and extends the scope of this inquiry to determine who bears the primary responsibility for the destruction of Babylon through apocalyptic fire.
Michael	I've been waiting for this point to be raised for a long time. After all, they can't go on forever pretending that we Germans are the sole culprits.
Raphael	This is Judgment Day we're setting into motion; we mustn't forget our dear neighbors to the East.
Jonah	I object to the term "apocalyptic" fire. I'd hate to see the *Lord* (He motions to the ceiling and makes a short pause for effect) implicated even

before we start our inquiry.

Judge Objection sustained. Let us merely say "fire." This term includes not only the total destruction of entire sections of cities within a few hours, but also the all too familiar phenomenon of death through asphyxiation, suffocation, and burial alive of countless thousands of human beings.

Woman The outcome's a foregone conclusion. You'll arrive at the same stupid result: we're responsible—we who were scared stiff ourselves. What stupidity!

Jonah Some people just never learn. Oh yes, I know: the twentieth century can't do wrong. Why can't it be that man is so stupid, so short-sighted? No prejudices, please.

Man Oh no, I still say there's a political motive behind all this. The Queen's guilty! She ordered the furnaces built!

Queen (Snapping at the AVERAGE MAN) You're guilty! You, the average man! I didn't place a single brick, I didn't carry a single log of fire-wood.

In the meanwhile the three ARCHANGELS have held a quiet huddle. Now GABRIEL steps forward.

Scene Seven

Gabriel	May I have the floor, Your Honor.
Judge	Certainly.
Gabriel	In the name of the three Archangels I wish to make the following declaration! For several thousand years we, the Archangels, have observed with ever increasing chagrin that those who wield political power have been encroaching upon our duties in shameless fashion. We, the Archangels, have been designated to act as the guardians of nations...
Michael	I, Michael, as guardian angel of Germany...
Raphael	(To MICHAEL) It's all right. Let *him* speak.
Gabriel	Yet who prevents us, the appointed leaders of the heavenly hosts, from guarding the nations so that they won't fall prey to need and death and despair? The presumptuous, brazen powers-that-be of the earth! The well-founded suspicion exists among us that the ultimate guilt, the arch-responsibility for the misfortunes of nations falls upon the crowned heads. What crass insolence to

prevent us, the Archangels, from exercising our holy and blessed duties. Power is evil, forever evil...

Raphael   Therefore we move that the inquiry be directed against the Queen...

Queen   Well, this I'm really anxious to hear.

Jonah   I share the Archangel's opinion. The servant merely basks in his master's glory. When the aristocracy becomes degenerate through debauchery and drunkenness, the people turn into a rabble. Nineveh's sins stank to high heaven when harlotry and decadence held sway in the halls of the palace; it was saved when news reached the people that the king had shed tears of remorse over the sins, and over the prophesied destruction of the city. Who persisted in sending us to seas in submarines when the radar- and sonar-equipped hunters made success and safety impossible?

Gabriel   Who prolonged the war until my beautiful Dresden collapsed into a heap of rubble and dust?

Michael   And who ordered those decent Amis to drop their bombs around the clock?

Raphael   Who chased millions of refugees into the barren countryside? Who gave the orders that were to drive them from the land of their forefathers?

A big commotion ensues, in which ALL, with the exception of JONAH and JUDGE, participate. Boos and hooting, shouts and whistling.

All   Down with the rulers! Revolution!

ALL point at the QUEEN.

All   She did it! She gave the orders!

Judge   Enough! That's enough! Order in the Court!

When semblance of order is re-established he turns to the QUEEN.

Judge   The people have identified you as the original cause of these excesses.

Queen   All right! I identify myself with that. All right! I was the Queen, I ordered the furnaces built, I corrupted the souls of my subjects, I tortured people to death, I tricked them into wars, I ordered saturation bombings of cities! I'm German, English, French, American, Japanese, Russian, Babylonian, Arabian! Do you really believe all that? Do you really believe I could have done all that? Do you honestly believe a human being is capable of all that?

Jonah   Your Honor! I've been saying it all along: the people of every century have never been at a loss for excuses. This is particularly true of the twentieth century. In one flash they erase entire cities with their cursed atom bombs; they permit millions of people of another denomination to die in gas chambers, and then they simply tell us: it's monstrous, it's inhuman, therefore it can't be true! But Intercontinental missiles do exist, supersonic sound has been attained, submarines are nuclear-powered, and still lay helpless on ocean floors. (To the AUDIENCE and the actors on stage) What sort of delusions do you labor under? Afterwards you tell us something you consider very smart and intelligent. You say it's the inevitable evolution of technology, the evolution of power! (To the QUEEN) And what sort of delusions do *you* labor under? Even though you're the Queen of Babylon tonight— and the Queen of the South—we're not re-enacting an old fairy tale.

Queen   Michael, guardian angel of all Germans! I beseech you, protect me from the raving prophet. Can't you offer extenuating circumstances? You're so well versed in the Bible.

Michael   (Thinking for awhile) Oh yes, this might do. (To JONAH) My dear prophet, how does his quotation from the prayers of your colleague Daniel strike you? "Blessed be the name of the Lord from everlasting to everlasting, for wisdom and might are his."

Jonah   But that hardly excuses the lack of wisdom and might in *human* beings. (To JUDGE) What is your opinion?

Judge   (Rising from his seat, he begins to pace back and forth agitatedly) It is terrible! Terrible! Once again the daughter of man is trying to seduce the angels, just as she did in olden times, primeval times, when sin was rampant and naked and all powerful.

Michael   I'm merely quoting from the Holy Scriptures. Now I'm coming to the point: "He changeth the seasons and times, he removes kings and sets up kings; he gives wisdom to the wise, and

	knowledge to those endowed with understanding."
Jonah	So what is your point?
Gabriel	(Suddenly greatly agitated) Oh, now I understand! Now I understand what Michael's trying to tell us. It's absurd! No—not absurd, dreadful! I don't dare say it.
Judge	What don't you dare say?
Gabriel	(Somewhat calmer) First of all, it's madness to build furnaces of fire, to exterminate six million people...
Raphael	To turn untold millions into homeless refugees...
Gabriel	It is madness to wipe out entire cities merely to win a victory; to construct atom bombs and to turn the surface of the globe into a landscape of craters.
Queen	Yes, that is true! It was madness, drunkenness!
Michael	In his Revelations, in the eighteenth chapter, John also mentions drunkenness. Let me think for a moment. —Oh yes. Listen: "She is fallen! Mighty Babylon is fallen! She has become the haunt of demons, and a dungeon for every unclean spirit. For drinking the wine of her immorality all the heathen have fallen; the kings of the earth have joined in her idolatry, and the merchants of the earth have grown rich from excessive luxury!"
Merchant	(Moaning aloud, he covers his face with his hands) Oh, my God! Oh, my God!
Michael	"Then I heard another voice from heaven say, come out of here, my people, so that you may not

share in her sins and suffer from her plagues!"

Woman Where could we have gone? We had such a beautiful apartment.

Man In the end the devil got it anyway.

Judge (To QUEEN) Do you consider drunkenness an extenuating circumstance? What nonsense! Who forced you to drink? Who enticed you to commit these atrocities? But even then it takes two: the tempter, and the one who permits herself to be tempted.

Raphael Perhaps a parable will help. The meaning of an image is at once poetic and divine.

He approaches the JUDGE with a sly expression.

Raphael Imagine a field freshly sewn with seeds. The peasant has completed his task, the seeds sprout and, so to speak, also complete their task. But there's no rain, no sun. Not a very rare occurrence these days. So the crop withers, there is crop failure. The people become needy— tempted, I meant to say—to act evilly, sneakily, viciously. Hunger invariably does that to people. You still remember, don't you? Tell me: who is still indebted to the seed?

Judge Who is still indebted? What did Michael say just before? "He gives wisdom to the wise, and knowledge to those who are endowed with understanding!"

Raphael Suppose he doesn't give? Who, then, owes the world wisdom and knowledge? Who, then, permits it to lapse into drunkenness?

Jonah   Raphael!

Michael (Running to the JUDGE) It is written in the Book
         of Job: "Behold: if He destroys, it cannot be
         rebuilt; when He shuts up a man, it cannot be
         reopened; if He sent them forth, they overturn the
         earth. The misled and the misleader are His!"

Judge   What is the meaning of all this? Whom do you
         mean? Of whom do you speak? Who is this He?

Queen   He is the very last to know!

All   (Excepting JUDGE and JONAH) God is guilty!
         God is guilty! God is guilty!

Man   Amen!

Scene Eight

Jonah   God! That is nonsense!

Judge   God the guilty one? (To the MERCHANT) Do you believe that, too?

Merchant (Shrugging shoulders) I don't really know. Your Honor, do you find it possible to believe differently?

Jonah   And the others? (Looking at each in turn, he asks each)

You?

But all remain silent.

Jonah   Each of you screamed it at the top of your voices. (To JUDGE) You see, Your Honor, I told you before we even began. This is the twentieth century, the raving twentieth century! It's incredible. They're already knocking at the gates of hell, but *God* is guilty! I've known all along it's no use. No use...

Judge   (To all except JONAH) Now, folks, let's be sensible. You folks can't possibly believe that. I plead with you not to believe that. That's impossible.

Queen   The trial proved His guilt beyond the shadow of a doubt.

Judge   No! I must reject the manner in which evidence has been presented. I can't, I mustn't accept it. Not I...

Merchant Now you're guilty of the same mistake you cautioned others from making: you're revealing prejudices. Please, Your Honor, consider this calmly. Is there any reason why God shouldn't be guilty? As a matter of fact, I've been toying with the idea for quite some time...

Judge   You of all people! You who've survived without difficulty?

Merchant What do you mean, without difficulty? Do you think it's such a simple thing to survive?

Woman   God is guilty! That's true! True! True! I speak for all the mothers of the twentieth century! I speak in the name of all the innocent children who died in the last two wars. I speak in the name of those who froze to death while fleeing for their lives— people who were innocent of the atrocities committed—and whose corpses were thrown into the ditches along the roads. I speak in the name of all the children who, at an age where they should be playing on sunny playgrounds, had to face the horrors of their times. I speak in the name of children who died of hunger and sickness. I ask, where was the God we were taught to call Father? He has failed, just as this

Court must fail, because the children aren't here to accuse Him with their emaciated, decayed bodies, and with eyes hollow from hunger and terror. Can't you see them? Can you ever rid your memory of that image? Then join me in my cry: God is guilty! Guilty!

Wildly sobbing, she collapses on the bench.

Merchant (To the AUDIENCE) You who've survived the terror of the bombing raids, give us the remaining wretches! Give them to me! I haven't any more. He let them perish in the flames, burnt alive, helplessly stuck in molten asphalt. Oh curses! Curses! Curses!

Jonah (To JUDGE) That's the raving mad twentieth century.

Queen (Having overheard this last remark) No! It's the voice of the rabble that must be ruled with furnaces of fire, that must be forced to pray to idols because they enslave without mercy! I was obliged to tame wild beasts! Who dares call me a sinner because I used a whip? Seat yourself upon a throne; from up high you get to know mankind. Every village, every hamlet, is chock full of whores and thieves and drunkards. For a tiny reward brother betrays brother. Only fire and sword keep them in line! Build *more* furnaces!

(Turning to the AUDIENCE) It is for you that I need them! Where were you when millions were gassed? While fighting men of all nations remain locked in mortal combat, while prisoners of war still suffer privations, where are you? Counting profits, and concerned with your pleasures and comforts only.

(To the MERCHANT) You mongrel dog! I know all about you! You built yourself a beautiful store to make money. In the rubble they found human remains. And twenty years ago, on the very same spot, stood the store of David Mayer, later gassed at Auschwitz!

(To the AUDIENCE) Where twenty years ago you demolished the apartments of Jews and desecrated their synagogues and beat them, you now have your neon signs, you mongrels, and when Christmas comes, one tree standing next to another. Peace on earth! (Laughs) Just let me hold the reins once more...!

Laughing shrilly, hysterically, she breaks down, and JONAH leads her to the bench.

Jonah	Calm yourself, please, calm yourself.
Man	Your Honor, may I have the floor!
Judge	(Wearily) If you must, go ahead.
Man	Look at me, gentlemen, as I stand before you. A man? The crowning glory of the creation? (Laughs) A wreck! I'm an average man, the man of the street. No, the man *in* the street. Do you know what that means? Goose stepping! Goose stepping for a dozen years! Goose stepping, goose stepping, goose stepping. I've suffered hunger and thirst and the fear of death. I was a man broken in body and spirit when they

discharged me before the end of the war. The First War, that is. Did the fatherland grant me my well-earned rest? Like that gentleman here...

(Pointing at the MERCHANT) I, too, was dealt harsh blows in my old age. The Second War robbed me of my two sons. My beloved wife died from grief and privations, for we were driven from the home of our fathers. Our daughter, a lovely, pale, angelic little girl, died of typhoid. She was to have been the joy and solace of our old age. I ask you, can any man have sinned so terribly that he must bear such a burden?

(Pausing briefly, then) You're all silent, all of you, even the Archangels. With my last ounce of strength I dragged myself here, for only the burning desire to *get even* keeps me going. (To JUDGE) Your Honor! If this court is just, you must pronounce just sentence. If you can locate the God whom I lost in the course of two wars, condemn Him, as I am condemned, to lead the life of man on earth. Let Him wander about, as I must wander about, without a home to rest His weary head. Let Him feel the pain, as I feel the pain, of having lost His son. Let Him suffer, as I had to suffer, hunger and thirst and the fear of death. Then, perhaps, in future centuries, He will govern more wisely...

Merchant (Eagerly shaking the AVERAGE MAN'S hand) Your faith is not unique. I know how it is...

Jonah   You see, Your Honor, the twentieth century. I warned you against having anything to do with these people.

Judge   I must admit it is highly irregular for a witness to pronounce sentence. However, the Court will take cognizance of his remarks. I'm beginning to realize myself that the evidence against the unknown defendant is overwhelming.

Queen   If anyone, by virtue of rank and position, is entitled to pronounce judgment, it is I. Except you, of course, Your Honor. (Slightly inclines her head to JUDGE) A short while ago, in this very room, grave accusations have been leveled against me. No one is happier than I to find that the true circumstances have been brought into the open. The higher one's position, the more painful the fall, if fall one must. We have heard the accusations of the father, the accusations of the mother. What are they compared to my own sufferings? The mother lost her children, the father his family and home. But I, a sovereign, lost an entire country. My capital, rich, happy, golden Babylon, collapsed into rubble and dust within one hour. Once the rulers of the earth paid me homage; here I must suffer accusations of harlotry and wickedness. Yes, I ordered the furnaces built! It had to be! I was compelled to do it! My position demands that I lead my people, give them laws to preserve order among them, for man left to himself is chaos. In order to enforce the laws I had to be severe. I was forced to kill in order to preserve life. Who created man in such fashion that only the threat of death and terror make him manageable? God! Who arranged the world in such fashion that kings must commit greater sins than other mortals? God! Who forces us to keep our nations alive by leading them up to the altar to be bled white? God! Who transforms the clear-cut actions of the princes into terrible ambiguity? God! Who transforms our crowns of gold into crowns of thorns? There is only one answer, though everyone seems wary to pronounce it. Only one verdict is possible: God must become king of kings! He must be forced to make laws for man! He must wear the crown of thorns, and from a place of high honor he must be thrust into damnation. This I say, in the name of those who ever wore a crown!

Judge   (After a brief silence) Archangels! You have heard the accusations. I command you to inform God of the verdict. How shall we phrase it?

Man   God shall become a human being, a wanderer on the earth, deprived of his rights, homeless, hungry, thirsty, in constant fear of death.

Woman   He shall be born to a woman, somewhere along a country road, and the moans of other poor creatures shall ring in his ears day and night. He shall be surrounded by the feeble, the sick, the filthy, by people bearing marks of leprosy. Rotting corpses shall bar His path. He shall know what it means to die. He, himself, shall die!

Man   And lose a son, and suffer the agonies of fatherhood.

Queen   And when at last He dies, he shall be disgraced

and ridiculed.

Judge   Do you consider this sentence to be just and proper? Does no one object?

Jonah   Of course not.

Judge   (Touching each as he calls his name) Michael! Gabriel! Raphael! You, you the spokesmen of God, what say you?

All three shake their heads in silence.

Judge   Go then! Inform Him of the verdict rendered by a tortured humanity.

Gabriel   I, Gabriel, shall go to a country ruled by cruel, parasitic men, a divided land occupied by a foreign power. I shall go to a virgin named Mary. She shall bring God into the world, under suspicion of shame—and as a Jew!

Michael   I, Michael, shall order the Heavenly Hosts to let Him walk the earth unprotected. When He falls to His knees, when the curse of being a man sends sweat dripping from his brow like drops of blood, I shall grant Him sufficient strength only that He may go on suffering, shall console Him as He consoled the faithful, putting them off with promises so that they can bear more suffering.

Raphael   I, Raphael, shall be present when He sinks into death, and I shall stand by His grave, and be the horror's holiest witness that God is dead!

Judge   Oh, what have I done? I condemned God! Never again shall I sit in Judgment. Human beings may rightfully fear my decisions. (To the

ARCHANGELS) I shall go with you. I can no longer be judge!

HE and the ARCHANGELS exit. JONAH now takes the JUDGE'S place in center stage, while all the other actors move to the opposite side of the stage.

Scene Nine

Jonah   (After a lengthy pause) What do you think you really have accomplished, people of the twentieth century? Do you think you have done something particularly bold, have made a new discovery? It is just a rediscovery! We could continue in modern fashion now, show you something very appropriate by means of a projector and screen. It would probably be as effective as the afore-mentioned mene tekel, particularly if we employed the creations of top artists—Durer's woodcut of the Birth of Christ, for example, and Grunewald's painting of the Crucifixion. But good taste prevents us from showing you the actual execution of the verdict. You know that it was carried out, and you know in what fashion. (He pauses briefly) There is little else for us up here on stage to do, since it is a reasonable assumption that you, to a certain degree, are somewhat involved in your own thoughts. (Again pauses briefly) As you might have noticed, all the remaining actors have felt that something has

69

transpired, and for that reason they have changed places. Miss.... (He names actress playing QUEEN by her real name) Will you kindly tell us what you're trying to indicate by this change of place?

Queen   Simply this: a human being can be anything in his or her lifetime, enact one role or another. Man only has to make the proper decision. (Brief pause) Now we're no longer Babylonians, but the people of Nineveh and Sheba who, it was prophesied, will rise with the men of this generation at the Judgment, and no sign will be given it but the sign of Jonah.

Woman   Therefore we had to omit the Sign of the Manger and the Sign of the Cross.

Man   But the earth is filled with suffering mothers...

Merchant   And crosses, so many crosses.

Queen   But the reawakening of half-forgotten memories holds hardly enough promise for the men of this generation.

The STAGE MANAGER enters.

Stg. Mgr.   Which is the reason why the author has inserted a motto at the head of this script:

(She reads) "The Queen of the South will rise with the men of this generation... (Pointing at the MERCHANT) at the Judgment and will condemn them, for she came from the very ends of the earth to listen to Solomon's wisdom, and there is more than Solomon here! Men of Nineveh will rise with the men of this generation (Pointing at

	MERCHANT again) at the Judgment and will condemn it, for they repented at Jonah's preaching, and there is more than Jonah here!"
Jonah	(To the AVERAGE MAN and WOMAN who are standing together) Yes, yes, Nineveh! Those were wonderful days when your city was still undamaged. I came to you, and for three days I wandered through your beautiful streets and squares, and admired the mighty edifices and neat little homes, for never before had I been in Berlin—Nineveh, I meant to say! And then I told you how God had filled me with fear upon fear while I was at sea, until finally I was lost in the terrible blackness inside the whale.
Woman	And you asked, "do you love your city?"
Man	And we said, "Yes, from the bottom of our hearts."
Woman	And then you asked, "do you love your children?"
Man	And we said...
Merchant	(Interrupts, deeply moved) ... more than anything in the world!
Woman	And then you said, "weep for your city, for there are only forty more days left, and Nineveh will be destroyed."
Queen	And this news reached the palace. You told us of your own godless ways, and how you had to pass through hell before returning to God. So I ordered...
Man	...everyone to join in a fast...

Woman ...and we tore our luxurious gowns and sprinkled ashes on our heads, for we knew the end was near.

Man Yes, it was a stern ordinance.

Queen My husband, the king, and I abandoned all pride and vanity and discarded our crowns, for we knew we were in the wrong, and that Jonah was right.

Jonah For everything which tonight was brought before the bar of justice is the fruit of human viciousness. Man is always threatened by his fellow man.

Man And by his own guilt.

Merchant (To QUEEN) Then tell me, how did you manage to banish the threats inherent in man? For your city was spared, wasn't it?

Man Oh yes, it was spared. Nineveh the beautiful, she was spared. And Nineveh became even more beautiful, for the people repented and led godfearing lives. "God bless our Nineveh," was the friendly greeting from friendly lips. And where once had stood the furnaces of fire, no one, even secretly, rebuilt them. And where once atrocities had been committed, no colored lights and decorations were permitted to camouflage these places of horrible, but sobering memories.

Merchant You mean neon lights and Christmas trees?

Man If that's the way you like to interpret it, for yourself and for your country, it's all right with me. We searched ourselves...

Merchant (To QUEEN) How did it occur to you to proclaim the saving ordinance?

Queen I wish I could answer you that past experiences brought it about. But unfortunately man quickly forgets past experiences. Then it is well to take advice from proper sources. I had heard of the wisdom of Solomon, that powerful king of noble lineage. So I traveled across the desert, to learn from his wisdom, for wisdom is the essential requisite for a ruler.

Merchant And what did you learn?

Queen The wisdom of Solomon, even then, a thousand years before the birth of the Savior, was something so unique it was well worth crossing the great desert to hear it; even in those days when the world was foolish and hostile and lengthy travel dangerous. Solomon alone was wise, for he stood in awe of God.

Merchant He stood in awe of God?

Man The reason Nineveh was saved.

Woman We knew that man is always in the wrong before God.

Merchant Then what am I to do? On the site where my shop stands today human remains were found, and before that, other human beings suffered torture and shame and fear.

Jonah Condemn yourself, then god will acquit you.

Queen As the Judge condemned himself.

Merchant The Judge...? (Looking at everyone questioningly)

Jonah   He administered the law in place of God.

Merchant God condemned God! And we, we! accused him! Oh, never again, never!

The JUDGE enters.

Judge   Then, after all, it was not in vain.

Merchant No, it was not in vain. Let me assure you, it was not in vain!

Jonah   (To the AUDIENCE) If even for one man, it was not in vain. What about you, ladies and gentlemen?

Trick   Right you are, you up there! It was not in vain!

The ARCHANGELS return.

Michael   Ah, Mister Trick. Well, why don't you come up here? Join us! We're almost finished.

Raphael   (Pointing at the MAN IN THE AUDIENCE) He is also a trick.

Gabriel   One is tempted to say that our fate is a trick of God, to help us find the truth.

Jonah   (To AUDIENCE) Well, ladies and gentlemen, the fear of the Lord is the beginning of wisdom. A beginning, a terrible beginning perhaps, but better than none. If you enjoyed the tricks up here on stage, then please recommend our playlet to your friends... and enemies. You have a pretty good idea what shape the world is in. There is room for quite a few improvements. Or must we suffocate once more in a submarine? Our future lives will give the answer.

(Pointing at the side where the accusers of God had stood) One way—

(Pointing at the side where the people of Nineveh stand) or the other. I wish you a pleasant way home. Do not elbow your way to the exit. There is no need to rush. No bombs will fall... tonight!

THE END